DINO DOTS

DOUGAL DIXON

Stoddart

First published 1988 by
Stoddart Publishing Co. Limited
34 Lesmill Road
Toronto, Canada
M3B 2T6

Reprinted 1989 (twice), 1990

CANADIAN CATALOGUING IN PUBLICATION DATA

Dixon, Dougal.
    Dino dots

ISBN 0–7737–5222–6

1. Dinosaurs – Juvenile literature.   2. Drawing –
Juvenile literature.   1. Title.

QE862.D5D59 1988   j567.9′1   C88–094319–X

First published in Great Britain by
Simon & Schuster Limited 1988

AN EDDISON·SADD EDITION
Edited, designed and produced by
Eddison Sadd Editions Limited
St Chad's Court, 146B King's Cross Rd,
London WC1X 9DH

Phototypeset by Bookworm Typesetting,
Manchester, England
Printed and bound in Hong Kong

WHAT TO DO

Welcome to DINO DOTS.
If you are interested in dinosaurs you'll find lots to do and learn about your favourite animals. Here's how to start . . .

❶ **Find a soft pencil or a black, felt-tipped pen.**
❷ **Choose a puzzle.**
❸ **Find the start of the puzzle – there is a little arrow on the puzzle to help you find dot number 1.**
❹ **Join up the dots in the correct order.**
❺ **See what kind of animal you have drawn.**
❻ **Now look at the sticker sheet.**
❼ **Find the sticker that is the same shape as the animal you have drawn.**
❽ **Stick it down in the space indicated on your puzzle.**
❾ **Colour in the puzzle, using the colours in the sticker as a guide.**
❿ **Answer the quiz box questions by putting a tick in the box of your choice, and check your answers in the back of the book. Count up all your points and see if you are a DINO DOTS BRAIN BOX.**
⓫ **Finish off your picture by copying the name of the dinosaur, from the answer, into the space on the puzzle.**

WHAT IS A DINOSAUR?

All kinds of animals appeared and disappeared long before there were people on the Earth. Some of the most fascinating of these animals were the dinosaurs. They were reptiles, they lived on land, and they existed for a long, long time. Some of them were only the size of chickens, but some were among the biggest animals that ever lived. Some were fast runners and fierce hunters. Others were slow-moving, eating only plants. We know of about 800 different types of dinosaur from their fossils, but there are only a few that we know really well. Some of them we know only from an odd piece of bone. There were other types of reptile living at the same time. Some were shaped like dolphins and lived in the sea – others flew in the air like bats. These were not dinosaurs. All these reptiles lived between about 230 and 65 million years ago. Then they suddenly died out. We do not know what killed them. A meteorite may have crashed into the Earth and caused so much damage that the big animals could not survive, or maybe the climates changed too much. Anyway, 65 million years ago, the long success of the reptiles was over.

EARTH FORMED 4,600 MILLION YEARS AGO (MYA)

Life begins

THE TIME STEPS

The Earth is old – so old it is difficult to imagine. 4,600 million years takes some imagining! To make it easier, scientists divide up the Earth's history into periods, which are shown as a series of steps leading up to the present day. The Precambrian period was very long, lasting from the beginning of the Earth to 590 million years ago. The time since the Precambrian can be divided into shorter steps. Each of these shorter steps is defined by the animals and plants that lived then.

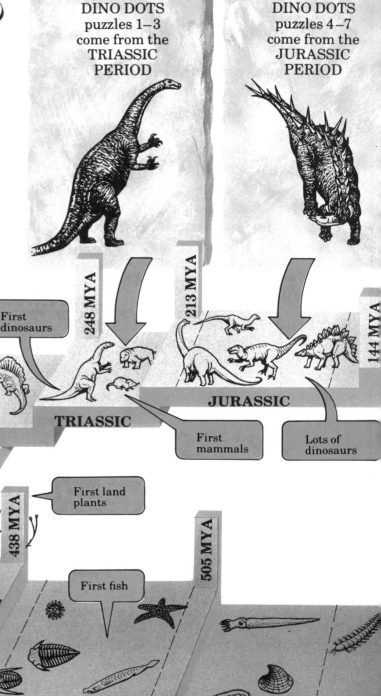

DINO DOTS puzzles 1–3 come from the **TRIASSIC PERIOD**

DINO DOTS puzzles 4–7 come from the **JURASSIC PERIOD**

248 MYA

213 MYA

144 MYA

All sorts of reptiles

First dinosaurs

286 MYA

First reptiles

PERMIAN

TRIASSIC

JURASSIC

First mammals

Lots of dinosaurs

360 MYA

CARBONIFEROUS

438 MYA

First land plants

First amphibians

Fish first to leave the water

408 MYA

505 MYA

First fish

DEVONIAN

SILURIAN

ORDOVICIAN

CAMBRIAN

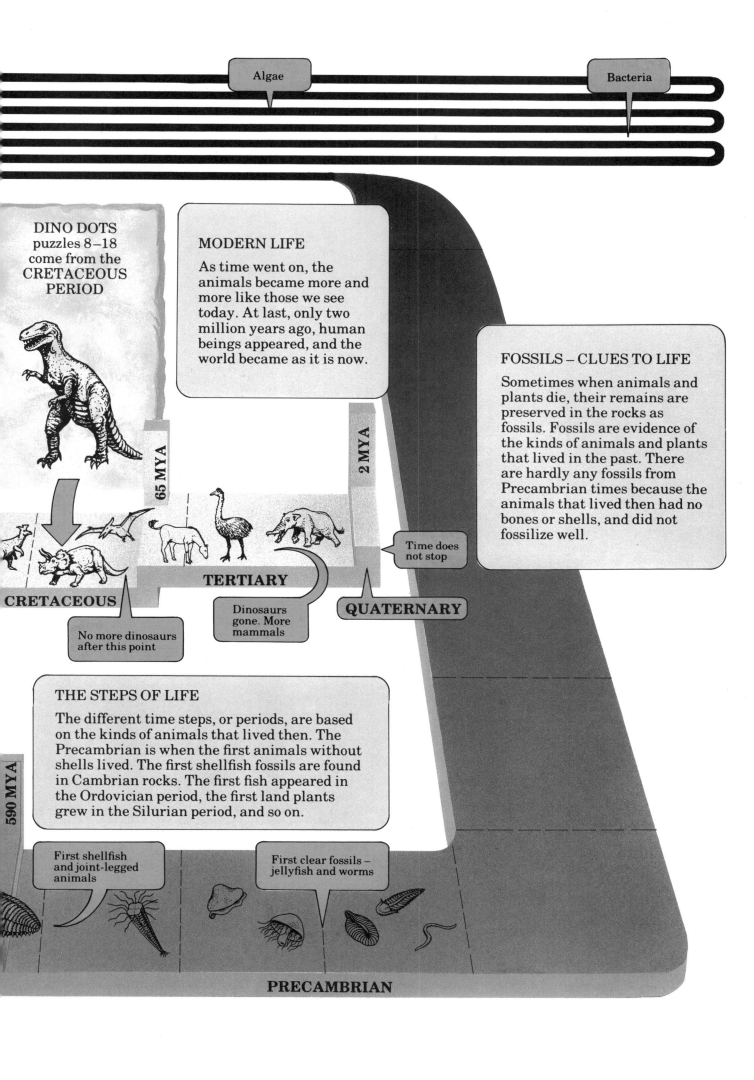

Algae

Bacteria

DINO DOTS
puzzles 8–18
come from the
**CRETACEOUS
PERIOD**

MODERN LIFE

As time went on, the
animals became more and
more like those we see
today. At last, only two
million years ago, human
beings appeared, and the
world became as it is now.

FOSSILS – CLUES TO LIFE

Sometimes when animals and
plants die, their remains are
preserved in the rocks as
fossils. Fossils are evidence of
the kinds of animals and plants
that lived in the past. There
are hardly any fossils from
Precambrian times because the
animals that lived then had no
bones or shells, and did not
fossilize well.

65 MYA

2 MYA

Time does
not stop

TERTIARY

CRETACEOUS

No more dinosaurs
after this point

Dinosaurs
gone. More
mammals

QUATERNARY

THE STEPS OF LIFE

The different time steps, or periods, are based
on the kinds of animals that lived then. The
Precambrian is when the first animals without
shells lived. The first shellfish fossils are found
in Cambrian rocks. The first fish appeared in
the Ordovician period, the first land plants
grew in the Silurian period, and so on.

590 MYA

First shellfish
and joint-legged
animals

First clear fossils –
jellyfish and worms

PRECAMBRIAN

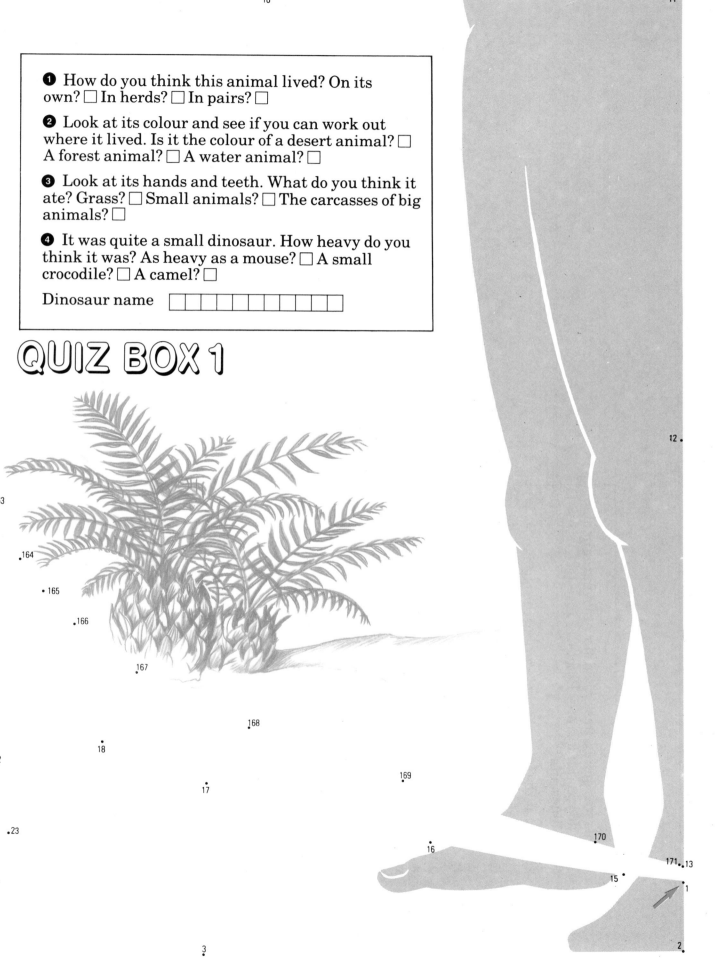

10

11

❶ How do you think this animal lived? On its own? ☐ In herds? ☐ In pairs? ☐

❷ Look at its colour and see if you can work out where it lived. Is it the colour of a desert animal? ☐ A forest animal? ☐ A water animal? ☐

❸ Look at its hands and teeth. What do you think it ate? Grass? ☐ Small animals? ☐ The carcasses of big animals? ☐

❹ It was quite a small dinosaur. How heavy do you think it was? As heavy as a mouse? ☐ A small crocodile? ☐ A camel? ☐

Dinosaur name ☐☐☐☐☐☐☐☐☐☐☐☐

QUIZ BOX 1

163

164

165

166

167

168

18

22

17

169

23

24

16

170

171 13

15

1

14

3

2

QUIZ BOX 2

❶ This was quite a heavy and slow-moving animal. What do you think it ate? Plants? ☐ Insects? ☐ Other dinosaurs? ☐

❷ Look at the strong front legs, and the big hands. How do you think this animal usually stood? On its back legs? ☐ On all four legs? ☐ Sometimes on its back legs and sometimes on all four legs? ☐

❸ See the desert landscape? How do you think this dinosaur survived? Staying in one place and digging for food? ☐ Travelling with the seasons from one watering place to another? ☐ Sleeping away the driest spells? ☐

❹ With such a long neck, where do you think it found most of its food? High up in the trees? ☐ Under stones? ☐ In pools? ☐

Dinosaur name ☐☐☐☐☐☐☐☐☐☐

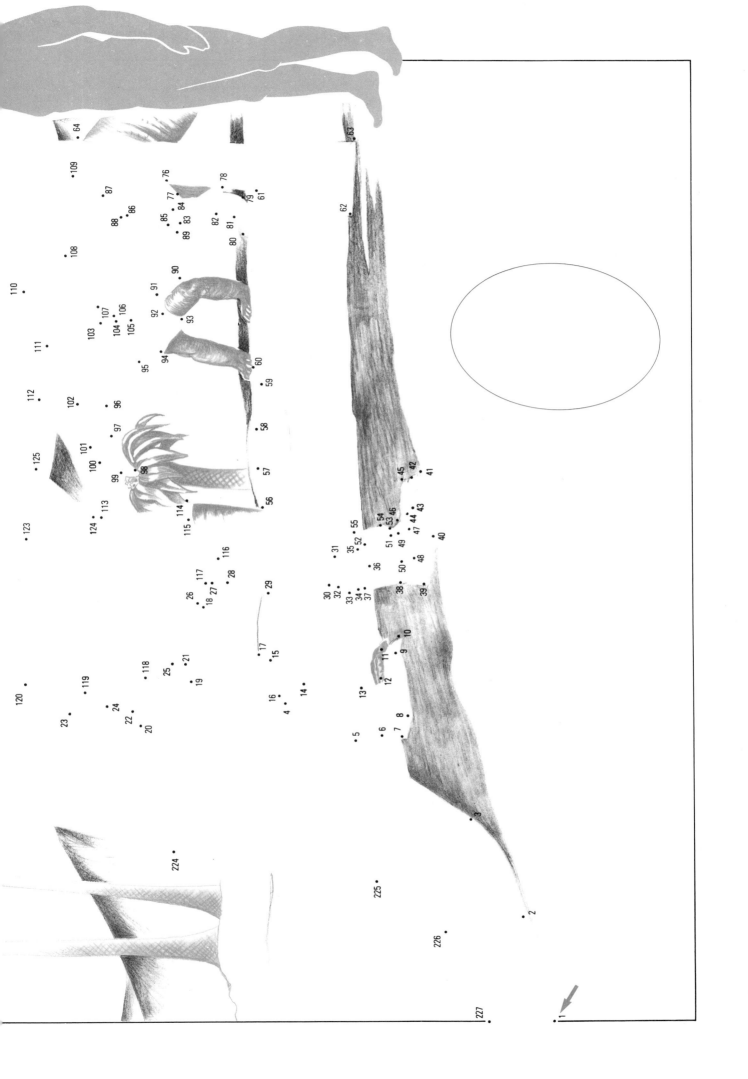

QUIZ BOX 3

❶ How did this small animal protect itself from bigger beasts? By running away? ☐ By biting back? ☐ With armour? ☐

❷ Did it walk on its back legs? Yes? ☐ No? ☐ Sometimes? ☐

❸ What would its long tail have been used for? For balancing its heavy armoured body? ☐ For fanning itself? ☐ As a whip-like weapon? ☐

❹ This dinosaur was a plant-eater. What kind of plants? Grass? ☐ Ferns? ☐ Flowers? ☐

Dinosaur name ☐☐☐☐☐☐☐☐☐☐☐☐☐☐☐

1 There are two animals here. What are they doing? Mating? ☐ Fighting? ☐ Playing? ☐

2 Which one was a meat-eater? The one standing on its back legs? ☐ The one at the front? ☐ Both? ☐

3 What did the animal at the front use the plates on its back for? Display? ☐ Armour? ☐ Controlling its temperature? ☐

4 What were the small front legs of the dinosaur at the back used for? Walking on? ☐ Holding on to the animals it fought? ☐ Scratching itself? ☐

Dinosaur name ☐☐☐☐☐☐☐☐☐☐☐☐

and ☐☐☐☐☐☐

QUIZ BOX 4

QUIZ BOX 5

❶ Look at the size of this dinosaur! How long do you think it was? As long as a blue whale? ☐ As long as a bus? ☐ As long as a tennis court? ☐

❷ Its head was tiny. How big do you think its brain was? As big as a sparrow's? ☐ As big as a cat's? ☐ As big as your own? ☐

❸ What would the long tail have been used for? As a weapon? ☐ As a support when it reached up into tall trees? ☐ For swimming? ☐

❹ It had very small teeth. How do you think it broke down all the plants that it ate? By swallowing stones to grind up the food? ☐ By eating only soft pond weed? ☐ By eating food already chewed by something else? ☐

Dinosaur name ☐☐☐☐☐☐☐☐☐☐☐

•177

180•

179•

•178

88•
89•
90• •87 •85
91•
•134
86• •84
92•
174•
135•
•133
136•
•132 •83
93•
137•
•141 •131 82•
145• 94• •79 76•
172• 138• •130
144• 142• 140 81• 80• 78•
163• •165 151• 143• 148• 139 99•
146• 147 •129 100
150• 95•
152• •149 96•
154• •153
171• •155 128• •98
161• 97•
103
•156
160• 104•
159• •157 127•
158• •126
125•
110• 109•
124• 121• •111 107
123• 120• •117 114• •112 108
122• 118• •115 •113
•119 •116
175•
173•
172•
164•
163• •165
162• 168• •166
167•
169•
170•
162•

QUIZ BOX ⑥

1 This dinosaur was closely related to another in the book. Which one does it look like? Puzzle 3? ☐ Puzzle 4? ☐ Puzzle 5? ☐

2 How big was it compared with its relative? Bigger? ☐ Smaller? ☐ The same size? ☐

3 What were the spikes on the tail used for? Defence? ☐ Display? ☐ Controlling its temperature? ☐

4 There is an extra pair of spikes on this animal. Where? On the nose? ☐ Above the shoulders? ☐ Above the hips? ☐

Dinosaur name

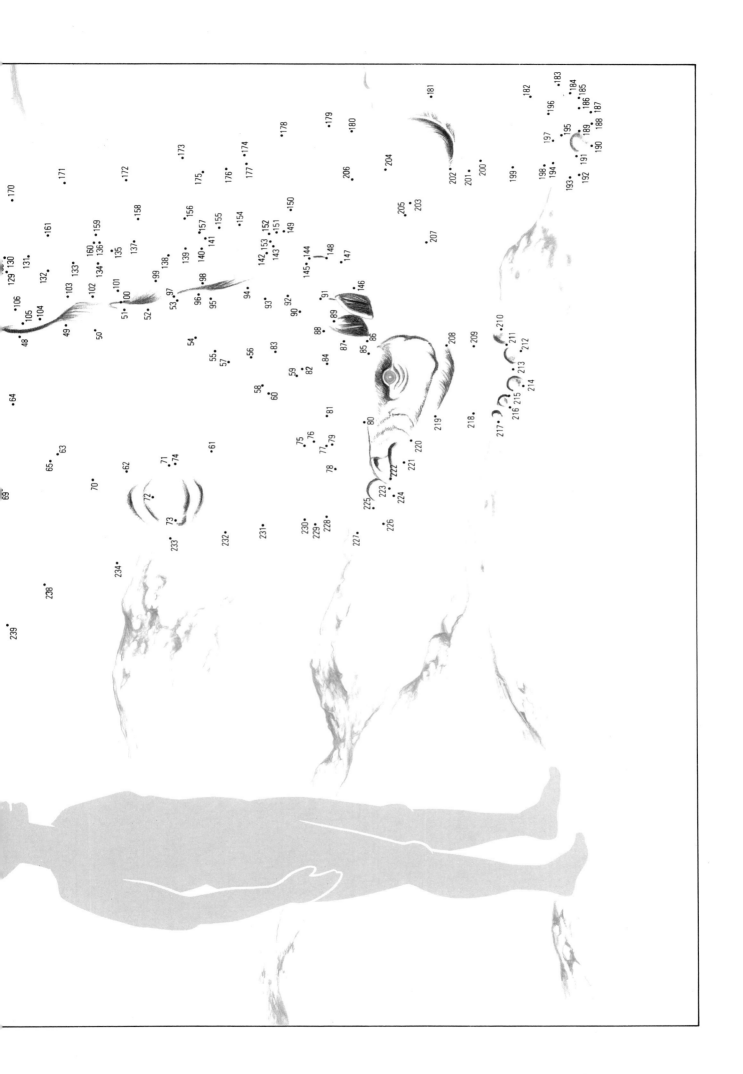

❶ This animal's shape is a half-way stage between a dinosaur and something else. A bird? ☐ A bat? ☐ A crocodile? ☐

❷ What were its dinosaur-like features? Its teeth? ☐ Its long tail? ☐ The fingers on its wings? ☐

❸ How big do you think it was? As big as a turkey? ☐ As big as a crow? ☐ As big as a robin? ☐

❹ What do you think it ate? Small things like insects? ☐ Or fruit? ☐ Or fish? ☐

Dinosaur name ☐☐☐☐☐☐☐☐☐☐☐☐☐☐

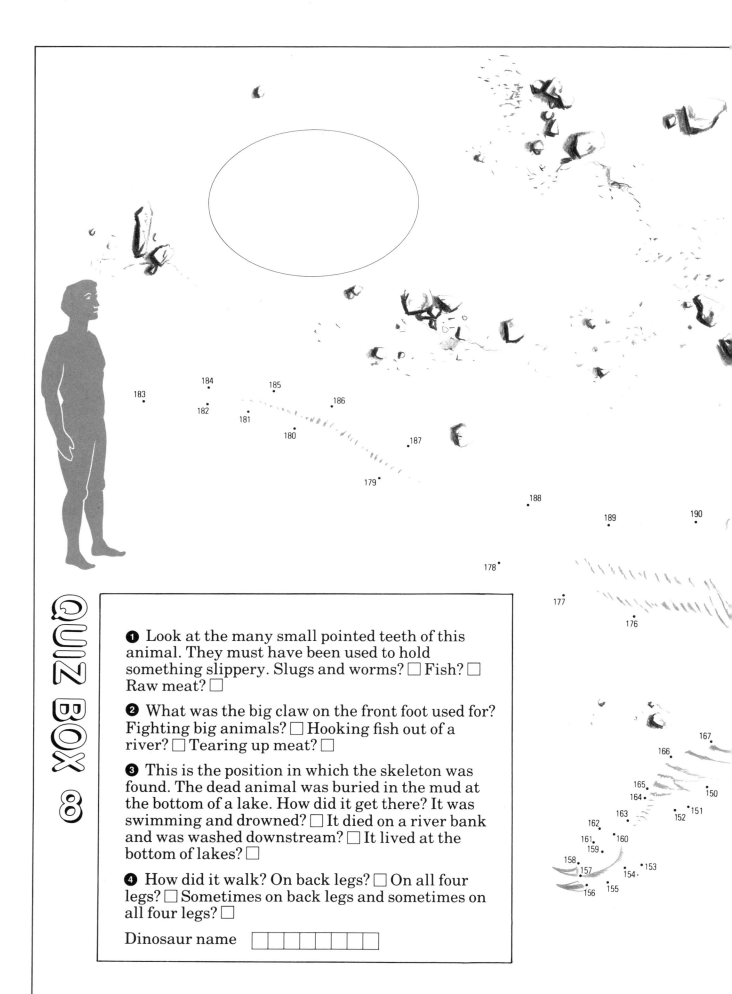

❶ Look at the many small pointed teeth of this animal. They must have been used to hold something slippery. Slugs and worms? ☐ Fish? ☐ Raw meat? ☐

❷ What was the big claw on the front foot used for? Fighting big animals? ☐ Hooking fish out of a river? ☐ Tearing up meat? ☐

❸ This is the position in which the skeleton was found. The dead animal was buried in the mud at the bottom of a lake. How did it get there? It was swimming and drowned? ☐ It died on a river bank and was washed downstream? ☐ It lived at the bottom of lakes? ☐

❹ How did it walk? On back legs? ☐ On all four legs? ☐ Sometimes on back legs and sometimes on all four legs? ☐

Dinosaur name ☐☐☐☐☐☐☐☐☐

QUIZ BOX 9

1 Here is a fierce creature. How do you think it killed its prey? By biting? ☐ By tearing it apart with the claw on its big back foot? ☐ By attacking with its strong fingers? ☐

2 The tail was very long. Was it stiff and straight? ☐ Curly and bendable? ☐ Spiked? ☐

3 The head was quite big. Was the brain small? ☐ Medium-sized? ☐ Big? ☐

4 How heavy do you think it was? As heavy as a young person? ☐ As heavy as a lion? ☐ As heavy as an elephant? ☐

Dinosaur name ☐☐☐☐☐☐☐☐

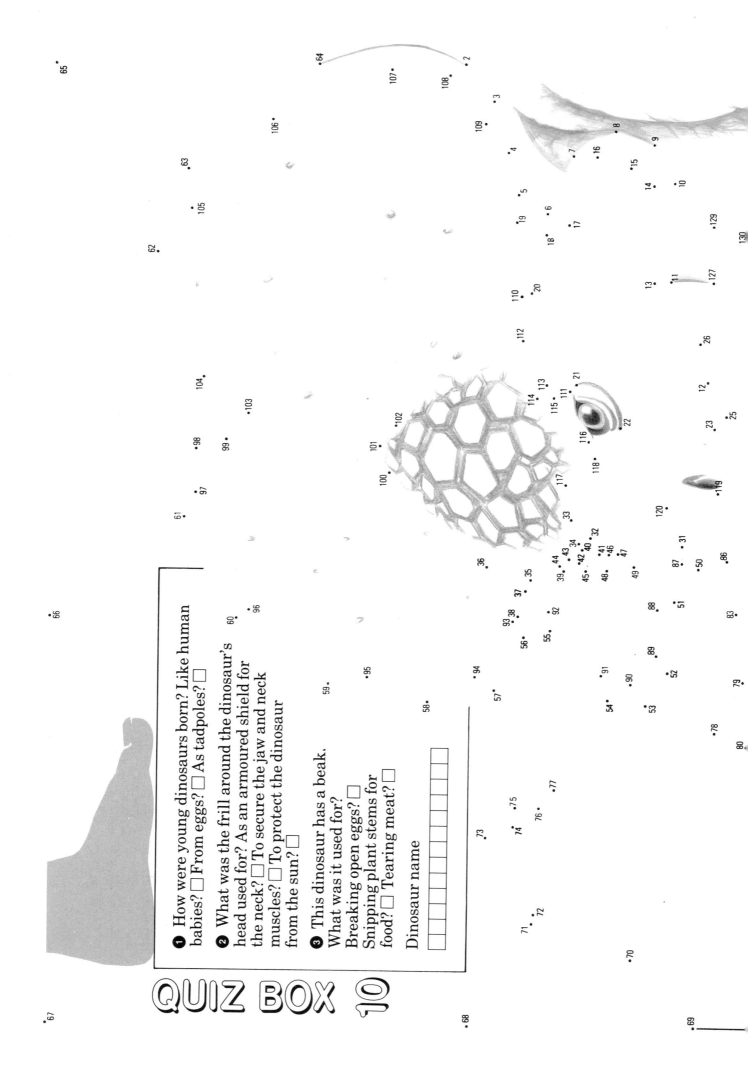

QUIZ BOX 10

1 How were young dinosaurs born? Like human babies? ☐ From eggs? ☐ As tadpoles? ☐

2 What was the frill around the dinosaur's head used for? As an armoured shield for the neck? ☐ To secure the jaw and neck muscles? ☐ To protect the dinosaur from the sun? ☐

3 This dinosaur has a beak. What was it used for? Breaking open eggs? ☐ Snipping plant stems for food? ☐ Tearing meat? ☐

Dinosaur name

☐☐☐☐☐☐☐☐☐☐☐

❶ Here is a big one! Look at its teeth. What do you think it ate? Other big animals? ☐ Insects? ☐ Ferns? ☐

❷ It had a huge sail on its back, made of upright bones and a web of skin. What was it used for? To control its temperature? ☐ To help it to swim? ☐ To signal with? ☐

❸ Without the sail it would look like another dinosaur. Which one? Puzzle 17? ☐ Puzzle 15? ☐ Puzzle 12? ☐

Dinosaur name ☐☐☐☐☐☐☐☐☐☐☐☐☐

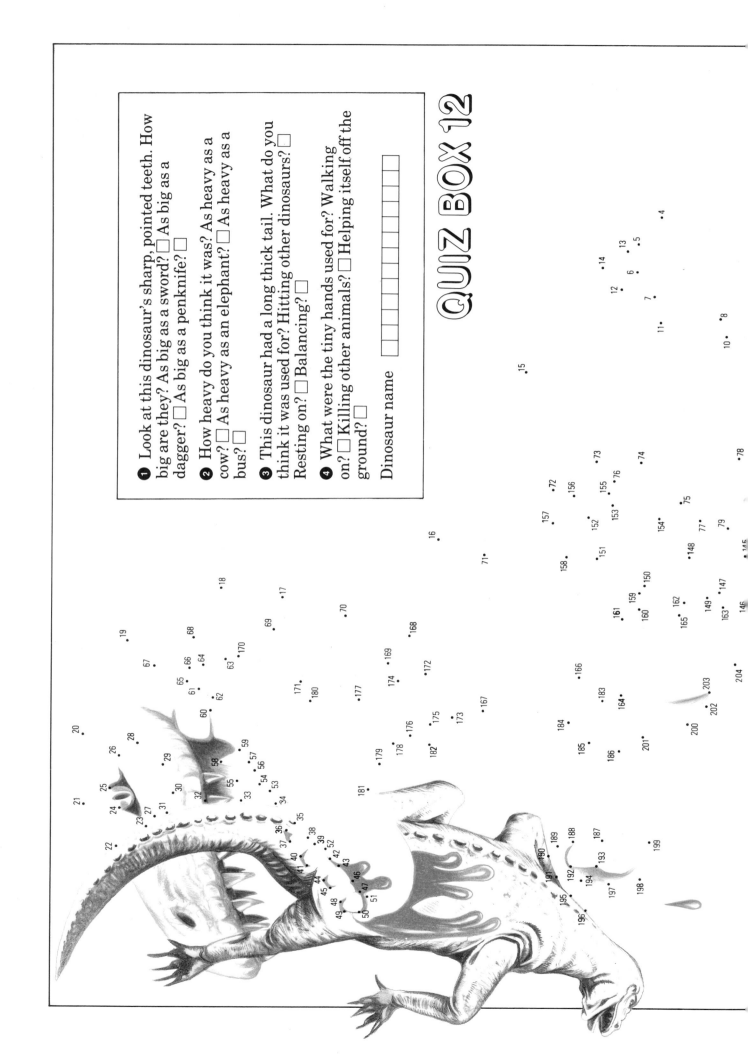

QUIZ BOX 12

1 Look at this dinosaur's sharp, pointed teeth. How big are they? As big as a sword? ☐ As big as a dagger? ☐ As big as a penknife? ☐

2 How heavy do you think it was? As heavy as a cow? ☐ As heavy as an elephant? ☐ As heavy as a bus? ☐

3 This dinosaur had a long thick tail. What do you think it was used for? Hitting other dinosaurs? ☐ Resting on? ☐ Balancing? ☐

4 What were the tiny hands used for? Walking on? ☐ Killing other animals? ☐ Helping itself off the ground? ☐

Dinosaur name ☐☐☐☐☐☐☐☐☐☐

134

229
228
135
227

136 141
143
140 142
138
139
137 144 179 180
230

226
225

224
188 189
223

222
145
187
181 185
190 191 221
192
220
197
146 193 219
178 186
177 184
182
200 194
198 196 218
173
183
172 200 195 216 217
176 174
201
147
202
175 171 215
203
148
149
170
151 153 154
150 152 155
204 209 210
206 213 214
205 211 212
207 208

156 169
162 168
157 167
158 161 165 166
159 163
160 164

109 111
108 112
110 113
107 125
124
114 119
106 116 123
115 118 121 122
120
95 117
94
96 97
105 99

98
102 100
104 103 101

231

1

2

3

QUIZ BOX 13

❶ What are these two animals doing? Scratching heads? ☐ Trying to see which is the stronger? ☐ Mating? ☐

❷ How did these animals live? On their own? ☐ In herds? ☐ In pairs? ☐

❸ Why were their heads so big and rounded on top? They were battering rams of solid bone? ☐ They protected the small brains from the heat of the sun? ☐ The animals were very brainy? ☐

❹ What do you think these animals ate? Plants? ☐ Insects? ☐ Other animals? ☐

Dinosaur name ☐☐☐☐☐☐☐☐☐☐☐☐☐☐☐☐☐☐

QUIZ BOX 14

1 This dinosaur's name means duck lizard. Why? Because it could quack? ☐ Because it had webbed feet? ☐ Because of the shape of its beak? ☐

2 Look at its broad flat teeth. What were they used for? Crushing shellfish? ☐ Grinding up plants? ☐ Breaking bones? ☐

3 Look at the sticker. It probably used its colour for camouflage. Where do you think it lived? In forests? ☐ In deserts? ☐ On open grassland? ☐

4 The broad head had a pouch on top of the nose. What for? For making croaking noises? ☐ To keep it afloat when swimming? ☐ To scare away enemies? ☐

Dinosaur name ☐☐☐☐☐☐☐☐☐☐

❶ This is another member of the duck lizard family. How does it differ from puzzle 14? It is bigger? ☐ It has a crest on the head? ☐ It lives in water? ☐

❷ What was the crest on the head used for? As an instrument for making noises? ☐ To circulate air in the skull? ☐ As a snorkel when swimming? ☐

❸ The duck lizard in puzzle 14 lived in what is now North America. This one lived in what is now China. What does that tell us? North America and China were joined at one time? ☐ Duck lizards could swim? ☐ Duck lizards could fly? ☐

❹ How can you tell that this dinosaur was a plant-eater? By the small mouth and pot-belly? ☐ The colour? ☐ The crest? ☐

Dinosaur name ☐☐☐☐☐☐☐☐☐☐☐☐☐☐☐

QUIZ BOX 16

1 What do you think all these spikes were for? Making the head look bigger to scare away enemies? ☐ Fighting? ☐ Protecting the back? ☐

2 When attacking, how would this dinosaur inflict the most damage? With the big horn on the nose? ☐ The little horns above the eyes? ☐ The beak? ☐

3 Its beak looks like that of a parrot. What was it used for? Picking berries? ☐ Pulling up roots? ☐ Chopping off tough plants? ☐

Dinosaur name

☐☐☐☐☐☐☐☐☐☐☐

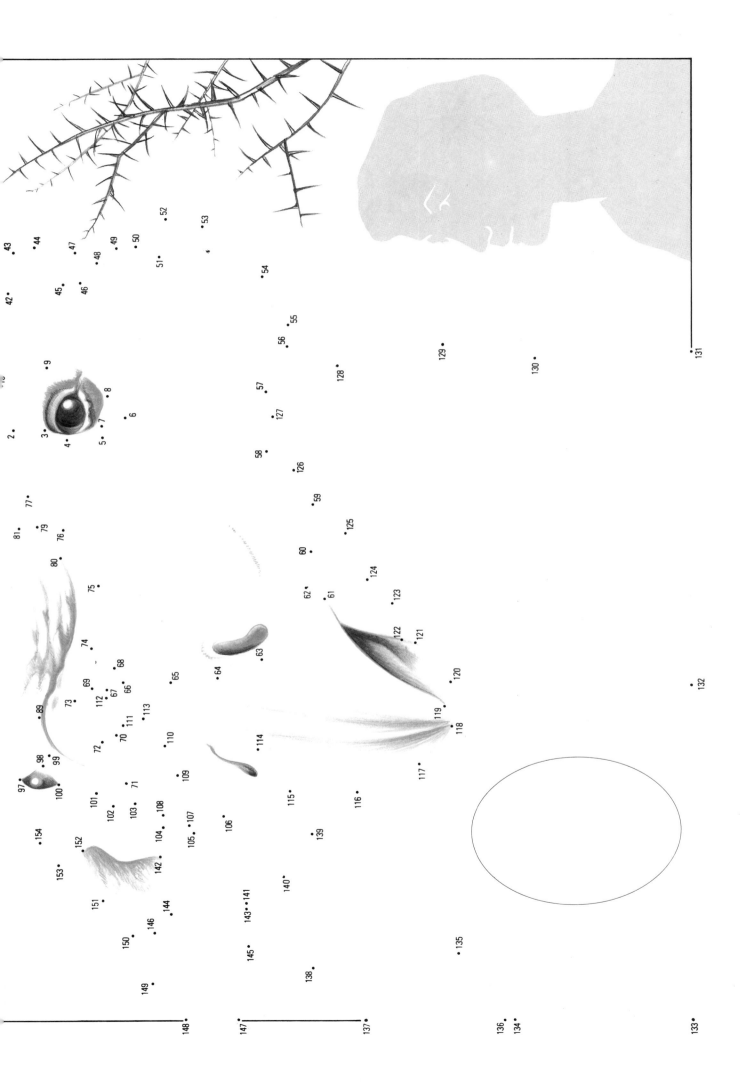

QUIZ BOX 17

❶ Look at the legs of this dinosaur. How did it move about? Was it a fast runner? ☐ Did it crawl slowly on all four legs? ☐ Did it climb trees? ☐

❷ How big was it? As big as a chicken? ☐
A turkey? ☐ An ostrich? ☐

❸ What kind of teeth did it have? Sharp, pointed teeth? ☐ Flat, crushing teeth? ☐ No teeth at all? ☐

❹ What did it eat? Small animals and insects? ☐
Fruit? ☐ Eggs? ☐

Dinosaur name ☐☐☐☐☐☐☐☐☐☐☐☐☐

QUIZ BOX 18

❶ Here is the biggest example of the horned dinosaurs. How many horns did it have? One? ☐ Two? ☐ Three? ☐

❷ What was the neck-frill used for? To protect the neck and shoulders? ☐ To support the strong jaw muscles? ☐ To control its temperature? ☐

❸ What are these two dinosaurs doing? Making friends? ☐ Fighting to see which is strong enough to lead the herd? ☐ Trying to pass round each other? ☐

❹ Why did the dinosaurs die out?

Dinosaur name ☐☐☐☐☐☐☐☐☐☐☐☐

QUIZ BOX ANSWERS

PUZZLE 1

Coelophysis
So–LOPH–iss–iss

❶ In a famous find of *Coelophysis*, dozens of skeletons were piled up. A **herd** of animals must have been caught in a sudden flood. 2 POINTS

❷ The skeletons were found in a bed of sandstone formed in a **desert**. 3 POINTS

❸ With its nimble fingers and sharp teeth, *Coelophysis* would have been able to catch and eat **small animals**. 2 POINTS

❹ *Coelophysis* was quite lightly built. The skeletons were about the size of a big lizard or a **small crocodile**. 2 POINTS

TOTAL SCORED [   ]

PUZZLE 2

Plateosaurus
PLAT–eo–SAW–rus

❶ Animals that eat **plants** have big stomachs to digest the tough plant material. 2 POINTS

❷ The front legs of *Plateosaurus* were strong enough for walking on. It probably spent **some time on its back legs and some time on all four legs**. 3 POINTS

❸ The only way for a big animal to survive in the desert is to **move from one watering place to another as the seasons change**. 3 POINTS

❹ As it could stand on its back legs it could reach its neck **high up into the tops of the trees**. It was the first animal that could do this. 2 POINTS

TOTAL SCORED [   ]

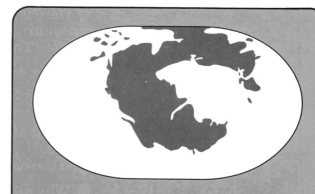

THE TRIASSIC PERIOD

At the beginning of the Triassic period all the continents of the world were united into one great supercontinent. We call this supercontinent Pangaea. Most of the interior of Pangaea was a long way from the sea, which meant that most of the land was covered in dry deserts. The dinosaurs first evolved in these Triassic deserts. The first mammals also appeared at this time, but they were small, insignificant animals.

How did you score?

PUZZLE 3

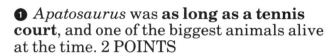

Scutellosaurus
Scu–TELL–o–SAW–rus

❶ *Scutellosaurus* was covered in **armour** to protect itself. Its name means 'lizard with little shields'. 2 POINTS

❷ As the back legs were longer than the front legs, *Scutellosaurus* **sometimes walked on its back legs**. 3 POINTS

❸ The tail was 2 ½ times the length of the body and must have been used **to balance the heavy armoured body** when the animal walked on two legs. 2 POINTS

❹ Grass and flowers had not evolved in the Triassic period. There were plenty of **ferns** for *Scutellosaurus* to eat. 3 POINTS

TOTAL SCORED ☐

PUZZLE 4

Ceratosaurus
Sir–AT–o–SAW–rus

Stegosaurus
STEG–o–SAW–rus

❶ These animals are **fighting**. 1 POINT

❷ *Ceratosaurus*, **standing on its back legs**, was a fierce meat-eater. 2 POINTS

❸ Some scientists think that the plates of *Stegosaurus* were brightly coloured and used for **display**. Others think they were covered in horn and used as **armour**. Yet others think they were covered in skin and used to **control its temperature**. Take full marks for any answer! 3 POINTS

❹ The front legs were used for **holding on to the animals it fought**. 2 POINTS

TOTAL SCORED ☐

PUZZLE 5

Apatosaurus
a–PAT–o–SAW–rus

❶ *Apatosaurus* was **as long as a tennis court**, and one of the biggest animals alive at the time. 2 POINTS

❷ The brain was very small – only about the size of **a cat's**. 2 POINTS

❸ The whip-like tail could have been used as a **weapon**. It was very strong at the base and would give **support** as *Apatosaurus* reached up into trees. Give yourself full points for either answer. 3 POINTS

❹ Heaps of stones near the skeletons tell scientists that *Apatosaurus* **swallowed stones to grind up the food**. 3 POINTS

TOTAL SCORED ☐

PUZZLE 6

Kentrosaurus
KEN–tro–SAW–rus

❶ *Kentrosaurus* was closely related to *Stegosaurus* **puzzle 4**, and lived in Africa, and skeletons of *Stegosaurus* have been found all over the world. Other relatives lived in China and Europe. 2 POINTS

❷ *Kentrosaurus* was one of the **smallest** in this family, about half the length of *Stegosaurus*. 2 POINTS

❸ The spikes that ran from the middle of the back down to the tail tip must have been used for **defence** against the meat-eating dinosaurs. 3 POINTS

❹ An extra pair of spikes **above the hips** helped to protect the back legs. 2 POINTS

TOTAL SCORED ☐

QUIZ BOX ANSWERS

Archaeopteryx
ARK–i–OP–terix

❶ *Archaeopteryx* represents the halfway stage between dinosaurs and **birds**. 1 POINT

❷ It still kept the dinosaur features of jaws with **teeth**, a **long tail** and **fingers on the wings**. Give yourself full points for any answer. 3 POINTS

❸ Fossils show that *Archaeopteryx* was about the size of a **crow**. 2 POINTS

❹ As it was small and active, and had sharp teeth, *Archaeopteryx* probably hunted **insects and other small creatures**. 3 POINTS

TOTAL SCORED ☐

Baryonyx
BAR–i–ON–ix

❶ *Baryonyx* had teeth like those of a **fish-eating crocodile**. Also, fish scales were found in its stomach. 3 POINTS

❷ It probably **caught the fish** with the huge hook of a claw. 3 POINTS

❸ The best dinosaur skeletons are found in lake deposits. This is because their bodies were **washed downstream** by rivers in flood. 2 POINTS

❹ *Baryonyx* probably spent much of its time on its long back legs. However, its front legs were very strong, and so it may have moved sometimes **on four legs and sometimes on two**. 2 POINTS

TOTAL SCORED ☐

THE JURASSIC PERIOD

In the Jurassic period Pangaea began to split and the separate continents started to drift apart. Shallow seas spread over the edges of the continents, and the Triassic deserts were replaced by jungles and forests. Many kinds of dinosaurs lived in the lush conditions of this period. They ranged in size from very large indeed to some that were as small as lizards or chickens. Swimming reptiles lived in the seas and flying reptiles appeared in the skies. The first birds appeared in the Jurassic period, and the mammals remained quite small.

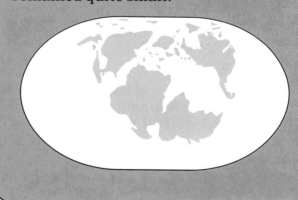

How did you score?

PUZZLE 9

Deinonychus
die–NON–i–kus

❶ The huge, powerful **claw on the back foot** was used for killing prey. 2 POINTS

❷ *Deinonychus* was able to stand on one leg and kill with the other, using a **straight stiff tail** as a balancing pole. 3 POINTS

❸ To be able to hunt and kill, and balance on one leg, *Deinonychus* must have had a **big brain.** *Deinonychus* and its relatives were the most intelligent of the dinosaurs. 3 POINTS

❹ *Deinonychus* was lightly built, weighing about 45 kilograms (100 lbs) – about the weight of a **young person**. 2 POINTS

TOTAL SCORED ☐

PUZZLE 11

Spinosaurus
SPINE–o–SAW–rus

❶ With teeth like those, *Spinosaurus* could only have been a meat-eater, and it probably ate **other big animals**. 3 POINTS

❷ *Spinosaurus* lived in quite a hot area. It probably used its sail to **control its temperature**, holding it into the wind to cool its blood. It was also used as a **signalling device**. Award yourself full marks for either answer. 3 POINTS

❸ With a length of 12 metres (40 ft), it was as big as *Tyrannosaurus,* **puzzle 12**, and looked similar. 2 POINTS

TOTAL SCORED ☐

PUZZLE 10

Protoceratops
pro–toe–SAIR–a–tops

❶ The **eggs** of this dinosaur were the first to be discovered, proving that dinosaurs were hatched from eggs. We now know of eggs and nests that belong to several other dinosaurs. 2 POINTS

❷ *Protoceratops* was one of the earliest of the frilled, horned dinosaurs. At first the frill was used to **secure the jaw and neck muscles**, but later it became an **armoured shield**. Give yourself full marks for either answer. 3 POINTS

❸ The horned dinosaurs all had beaks. These were used for **snipping the plant stems** on which they fed. 3 POINTS

TOTAL SCORED ☐

PUZZLE 12

Tyrannosaurus
tie–RAN–o–SAW–rus

❶ The saw-edged teeth of *Tyrannosaurus* were up to 18 centimetres (7 in) long, about the same as a small **dagger**. 2 POINTS

❷ It was one of the biggest of the meat-eaters. It was 12 metres (40 ft) long and weighed 6 tonnes, about as much as an **elephant**. 3 POINTS

❸ When *Tyrannosaurus* walked, the ground shook. It walked with its body held horizontally, and its stiff tail acted as a **balance**. 3 POINTS

❹ The little hands **steadied its great weight against the ground** when it rose to its feet. 3 POINTS

TOTAL SCORED ☐

QUIZ BOX ANSWERS

PUZZLE 13

Pachycephalosaurus
pak–ee–SEF–al–o–SAW–rus

❶ Male bone-headed dinosaurs like *Pachycephalosaurus* often head-butted each other, as goats do today, to **test which one was the stronger**. 3 POINTS

❷ They lived in **herds**, and the strongest male would become the leader. 3 POINTS

❸ Their skulls consisted of a thick mass of solid bone, used as **battering rams** during a head-butting contest. 2 POINTS

❹ They were **plant-eaters**, although they walked on their back legs like meat-eating dinosaurs. Plant-eaters have small mouths and cheek pouches for chewing. 3 POINTS

TOTAL SCORED [   ]

PUZZLE 14

Anatosaurus
a–NAT–o–SAW–rus

❶ The skull of *Anatosaurus* was broad and flat, like the **beak of a duck**. 3 POINTS

❷ The beak was used for scraping tough pine needles from branches. The flat teeth were used for **grinding up the tough plant material**. 2 POINTS

❸ *Anatosaurus* skeletons are found in rocks laid down in rivers. The dinosaurs probably lived in **forests** along river banks. 3 POINTS

❹ Some scientists think that the broad beak had an inflatable nose pouch that *Anatosaurus* could use to **make croaking noises**. 2 POINTS

TOTAL SCORED [   ]

PUZZLE 15

Tsintaosaurus
sin–TAY–o–SAW–rus

❶ It has a **crest on the head**. 2 POINTS

❷ The crest was formed by the nose bones and was probably used for **making noises**, and also **to circulate air in the skull** in hot weather. Give yourself full marks for either answer. 3 POINTS

❸ As the duck lizards lived only in Asia and North America, the two areas must have been **joined at one time**. 3 POINTS

❹ *Tsintaosaurus* could be mistaken for a meat-eater if it were not for the **small mouth, and the pot-belly** for digesting plant food. 3 POINTS

TOTAL SCORED [   ]

PUZZLE 16

Styracosaurus
sty–RACK–o–SAW–rus

❶ The spikes making a frill around the neck were at the wrong angle to be used as weapons, and they would not have covered much of the back as a shield. They would have been most successful at **making the head look bigger and more frightening**. 3 POINTS

❷ The **huge horn on the nose** was the most dangerous weapon that *Styracosaurus* possessed. Its best defence was to turn and face the enemy. 2 POINTS

❸ *Styracosaurus* used the strong beak for **chopping off tough plants**. 3 POINTS

TOTAL SCORED [   ]

How did you score?

THE CRETACEOUS PERIOD

In the Cretaceous period the continents were moving further apart. Forests of trees like oaks and willows appeared, and different dinosaurs lived on each continent. The dinosaurs disappeared at the end of this period and the mammals became dominant.

PUZZLE 17

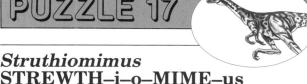

Struthiomimus
STREWTH–i–o–MIME–us

❶ These legs are for **running**! 1 POINT

❷ *Struthiomimus* was about the shape and size of an **ostrich**. 2 POINTS

❸ Even the head was like that of a bird. There may have been a beak, but there were **no teeth** in the mouth. 3 POINTS

❹ The mouth and the hands suggest that *Struthiomimus* may have eaten **small animals and insects, fruit** from the trees, or even **eggs** dug up from dinosaur nests. Award yourself full points for any of these answers. 3 POINTS

TOTAL SCORED ☐

PUZZLE 18

Triceratops
tri–SAIR–a–tops

❶ The name means 'three-horned head' and, unlike most other horned dinosaurs that had either a nose horn or a pair of horns above the eyes, *Triceratops* had all **three**. 3 POINTS

❷ The neck-frill was a strong piece of armour to **protect the neck**. 3 POINTS

❸ *Triceratops* lived in herds. These big males were **fighting to see which was strong enough to lead the herd**. 3 POINTS

❹ If you can think of any good answer to this one, award yourself a bonus of 10 points. None of the scientists can agree on it!

TOTAL SCORED ☐

Are you a DINO DOTS brain box?

How did you score? Fill in your puzzle totals and add them up to find your grand total.

Puzzle **1** Total scored ....   Puzzle **10** Total scored ....

Puzzle **2** Total scored ....   Puzzle **11** Total scored ....

Puzzle **3** Total scored ....   Puzzle **12** Total scored ....

Puzzle **4** Total scored ....   Puzzle **13** Total scored ....

Puzzle **5** Total scored ....   Puzzle **14** Total scored ....

Puzzle **6** Total scored ....   Puzzle **15** Total scored ....

Puzzle **7** Total scored ....   Puzzle **16** Total scored ....

Puzzle **8** Total scored ....   Puzzle **17** Total scored ....

Puzzle **9** Total scored ....   Puzzle **18** Total scored ....

TOTAL [ ]   TOTAL [ ]

GRAND TOTAL [ ]

The total number of points that you can score in this book is 180. You would be very clever indeed to get all of these.

If you scored more than 100 you are doing well. You can call yourself a DINO DOTS BRAIN BOX and wear the special 'gold' sticker.

If you scored more than 120 you did very well indeed – you can call yourself a DINOSWOT.

If you scored more than 150 you must be very clever and can call yourself a GRAND DINOMASTER.

THANK YOUS

Eddison Sadd Editions would like to thank the following: Andrew Farmer for the main illustrations; Anthony Duke for the dots; Amanda Barlow for artwork research and the maps; Sophie Wilkins for design help; and to Samuel Eddison (age 7), a special thank you for acting as consultant.

The following sources were used as reference for the illustrations: *The Illustrated Encyclopedia of Dinosaurs* by Dr David Norman, Salamander Books, London 1985; *The World of Dinosaurs* by Michael Tweedie, Weidenfeld and Nicolson, London, 1977; *A New Look at the Dinosaurs* by Alan Charig, British Museum (National History), London, 1985; *Claws*, a leaflet published by the British Museum (Natural History), London, 1987; *The Rise of Life* by John Reader, Collins, London, 1977; and *Collins Book of Dinosaurs* by Tom McGowen, Collins, London, 1976.